Derek Hicks.

MOY SAND AND GRAVEL

PAUL MULDOON

Moy Sand and Gravel

faber and faber

First published in 2002
by Faber and Faber Limited
3 Queen Square London WC1N 3AU

Photoset by Wilmaset Ltd, Wirral
Printed in Italy

A CIP record for this book
is available from the British Library

ISBN 0–571–21535–1

10 9 8 7 6 5 4 3 2 1

for Dorothy and Asher

Contents

Hard Drive 3
Unapproved Road 4
Moy Sand and Gravel 8
The Misfits 9
The Braggart 12
The Whinny 13
A Collegelands Catechism 15
Beagles 17
Tell 18
Guns and Butter 20
One Last Draw of the Pipe 21
Caedmon's Hymn 23
Paul Valéry: *Pomegranates* 24
Pineapples and Pomegranates 25
Winter Wheat 26
Herm 27
Whitethorns 28
Affairs of State 29
The Otter 30
John Luke: *The Fox* 31
Anthony Green: *The Second Marriage* 32
As 33
The Stoic 37
Famous First Words 39
The Grand Conversation 41
On 43
An Old Pit Pony 44
Summer Coal 45
The Loaf 47

The Outhouse 49
News Headlines from the Homer Noble Farm 50
The Killdeer 54
Horace: *Two Odes* 55
Eugenio Montale: *The Eel* 58
When Aifric and I Put In at that Little Creek 60
The Ancestor 62
Homesickness 63
Two Stabs at Oscar 65
The Breather 66
The Goose 67
A Brief Discourse on Decommissioning 68
The Turn 69
Redknots 71
Cradle Song for Asher 72
At the Sign of the Black Horse, September 1999 73

Acknowledgements

Acknowledgements are due to the editors of *The American Scholar, Avocado, Daedalus, Fulcrum, The Guardian, The Honest Ulsterman, The Irish Times, The Kenyon Review, Kestrel, The KGB Bar Book of Poems, London Magazine, The London Review of Books, magma, The Nassau Weekly, The New Delta Review, New Writing 8, The New York Review of Books, Notre Dame Review, The Observer, One Trick Pony, Ploughshares, Poetry Review, Quarterly West, The Recorder, River City, Samizdat, The Shop, Stand, The Sunday Times* (London), *Thumbscrew, Time's Tidings, The Times Literary Supplement, Translation Ireland, Troubadour, US1, Washington Square* and *The Yale Journal of Criticism*.

'The Ancestor', 'The Grand Conversation', 'News Headlines from the Homer Noble Farm' and 'When Aifric and I Put In at that Little Creek' first appeared in *The New Yorker*.

'Hard Drive' was privately printed by the Gallery Press in December 1998, 'John Luke: *The Fox*' in December 1999, 'Beagles' in December 2000, 'Horace: *Book* III *Ode* XVIII' in December 2001. 'Unapproved Road' was commissioned for *The Border: Personal Reflections from Ireland, North and South* (Oak Tree Press). 'Hard Drive' and 'Unapproved Road' appeared in *Unapproved Road*, a limited edition with intaglio prints by Diarmuid Delargy, published by Pied Oxen. The translation of 'Caedmon's Hymn' was made for Poems on the Underground, 'Paul Valéry: *Pomegranates*' for *20th-Century French Poems* (Faber and Faber), 'Horace: *Two Odes*' for *Horace, The Odes: New Translations by Contemporary Poets* (Princeton University Press) and 'Eugenio Montale: *The Eel*' for *20th-Century Italian Poems* (Faber and Faber). 'Herm' was included in *The Epic Poise: A Celebration of Ted Hughes* (Faber and Faber). 'Anthony Green: *The Second Marriage*' appeared in *A Conversation Piece* (Abbey Press), an anthology of poems about paintings in the Ulster Museum collection. A shortened version of 'As' was broadcast on RTE Television on 31 December 1999 ('Millennium Eve'), while 'The Stoic' was commissioned by the BBC World Service for 'The Lyrics'. 'News Headlines from the Homer Noble Farm' was included in *Last Before America: Essays and Poems in Honour of Michael Allen* (Blackstaff Press). 'Two Stabs at Oscar' was commissioned by Reading Borough Council to be incorporated in the Oscar Wilde Memorial Walk, while 'The Breather' was written for the 1999 Salisbury Festival and published in *Last Words* (Picador).

Moy Sand and Gravel

Hard Drive

With my back to the wall
and a foot in the door
and my shoulder to the wheel
I would drive through Seskinore.

With an ear to the ground
and my neck on the block
I would tend to my wound
in Belleek and Bellanaleck.

With a toe in the water
and a nose for trouble
and an eye to the future
I would drive through Derryfubble

and Dunnamanagh and Ballynascreen,
keeping that wound green.

Unapproved Road

I

When we came to the customs post at Aughnacloy, as at
   Cullaville or Pettigoe,
I was holding my breath
as if I might yet again be about to go

underwater ... The fortieth
anniversary of 1916 had somehow fizzled out, the New
   Year's Eve attack
on Brookeborough ending in the deaths

of O'Hanlon and South, while Dev was likely to bring
   back
internment without trial ... As we drew
level with the leveled shack

I was met by another black-coated, long fellow, though he
   wore a sky-blue
winding-cloth or scarf
wrapped round his mouth and nose, leaving only a slit for
   him to peer through.

II

'In the late fifties I was looking for a place,' he nestled his
   coffee cup on its zarf
and turned to me, thirty years later, in Rotterdam ...
'An ancestral place ... A place my ancestors knew as
   Scairbh

4

na gCaorach.' 'Scairbh na gCaorach,' I chewed on my
   foul madams,
'is now better known as "Emyvale"
though the Irish name means "the sheep-steeps" or "the
   rampart of rams".'

' "Rampart of rams?" That makes sense. It was the image
   of an outcrop of shale
with a particularly sheer
drop that my ancestors, the "people of the veil",

held before them as they drove their flocks from tier to tier
through Algeria, Mali and Libya all the way up to
   Armagh, Monaghan and Louth
with – you'll like this – a total disregard for any frontier.'

III

'Patrick Regan? A black-coated R.U.C. man was
   unwrapping a scarf from his mouth
and flicking back and forth from my uncle's license to his
   face.
'Have you any news of young Sean South?

The last I heard he was suffering from a bad case
of lead poisoning. Maybe he's changed his name to Gone
   West?'
I knew rightly he could trace

us by way of that bottle of Redbreast
under my seat, that carton of Players, that bullion chest
   of butter.
I knew rightly we'd fail each and every test

they might be preparing behind the heavy iron shutters
even now being raised aloft
by men carrying belt-saws and blow-torches and bolt-
  cutters.

IV

As he turned to me again, thirty years later in Rotterdam,
  the Tuareg doffed
his sky-blue scarf. 'Back in those days I saw no risk
in sleeping under hedges. As a matter of fact I preferred a
  thorn hedge to a hayloft

because – you'll like this – it reminded me of the
  tamarisks
along the salt route into Timbuktu.'
He crossed his forearms lightly under his armpits as if he
  might be about to frisk

himself, then smiled as he handed me the sky-blue
winding-cloth and a clunking water gourd.
'It had been my understanding that *Scairbh na gCaorach*
  means "the crossing of ewes"

for *scairbh* means not "a ledge" but "a ford" or, more
  specifically, "a shallow ford".'
And he immediately set off at a jog-trot down an
  unapproved road
near Aughnacloy or Swanlinbar or Lifford.

V

'It had always been my sense,' I hear him still, 'that the
    goat fades into the goad
and the spur fades into the flank
and the fastness fades into no fixed abode

and the Black Pig's Dyke fades into the piggy bank
and your Hams fade into your Japheths
and the point fades into the point-blank

and the Cristal fades into the crystal meths
where the ends somehow begin to fade into the means
and the sheugh fades into the shibboleth

and the timbre fades into the tambourine
and the quiddity fades into the *quid pro quo*
and – you'll like this, I know – the bourne fades into the
    boreen.'

Moy Sand and Gravel

To come out of the Olympic Cinema and be taken aback
by how, in the time it took a dolly to travel
along its little track
to the point where two movie stars' heads
had come together smackety-smack
and their kiss filled the whole screen,

those two great towers directly across the road
at Moy Sand and Gravel
had already washed, at least once, what had flowed
or been dredged from the Blackwater's bed
and were washing it again, load by load,
as if washing might make it clean.

The Misfits

If and when I did look up, the sky over the Moy was the
   very same gray-blue
as the slow lift
of steam-smoke over the seam
of manure on a mid-winter morning. I noticed the splash
   of red lead
on my left boot as again and again I would bend
my knee and bury my head in the rich

black earth the way an ostrich
was rumored to bury its head. My hands were blue
with cold. Again and again I would bend
to my left and lift
by one handle a creel of potatoes – King Edwards, gray as
   lcad –
mined from what would surely seem

to any nine- or ten-year-old an inexhaustible seam.
My father wore a bag-apron that read, in capital letters,
   'RICH'.
My own capital idea, meanwhile, had sunk like a lead
balloon. 'Blow all you like,' my father turned on me.
   'Talk till you're blue
in the face. I won't let you take a lift
from the Monk. Blow all you like. I won't bend.'

The Monk had spent twenty-odd years as a priest in South
   Bend,
his face priest-smooth except for a deep seam

in his left cheek. Fred Grew said something strange about
    how he liked to 'lift
his shirt-tail'. Jack Grimley chipped in with how he was
    'ostrich-
sized' because he once lent Joe Corr a book called *Little
    Boy Blue*.
When Fred Grew remarked on his having 'no lead

in his pencil', I heard myself say, cool as cool, 'I think
    you've all been misled.'
At which the RICHARDSON'S TWO-SWARD suddenly
    began to unbend
in that distinctive pale blue
lettering as the seam
of his bag-apron unstitched itself and my father turned on
    me again: 'That's rich,
all right. If you think, after that, I'd let the Monk give you
    a lift

into the Moy to see Montgomery bloody Clift
you've another think coming. I'll give him two barrels
    full of twelve-gauge lead
if he comes anywhere near you. Bloody popinjay. Peacock.
    Ostrich.'
All I could think of was how the Monk was now no more
    likely to show me how to bend
that note on the guitar – 'like opening a seam
straight into your heart' – when he played Bessie Smith's
    'Cold in Hand Blues'

than an ostrich to bend
its lead-plumed wings and, with its two-toed foot, rip out
    the horizon-seam
and lift off, somehow, into the blue.

The Braggart

He sucked, he'll have you know,
the tell-tale sixth toe
of a woman who looked like a young Marilyn Monroe,

her hubby getting a little stroppy
when he found them there in the back of that old jalopy.
Other papers please copy.

The Whinny

When he veered into the mirror to fix his collar stud
he heard the whinny
of a stallion at stud,
saw the egg-yellow gloss in the coat of a young ass or hinny

or a pit pony's glossy forelock
not unlike his own. A stable lad had already tried to pick
the lock
on his near hind hoof. All spick

and span then, turned out in the yard,
with the prepuce
of his yard
an unprepossessing puce,

he knew he'd have to buck
the trend
of these stud-collars, ordered from Sears Roebuck
at year's end

by one or other of his American 'aunts',
knew he'd have to surmount
the twits and taunts
of the stable lad who'd watched him mount

the dais, dressed to the nines,
to take the prize for Geography. 'You can't tell, I'll own,
the Pennines from the Apennines,
you little shit-your-knickers,'

he heard the pit pony vet
him over his own shoulder, his voice now full-blown,
now fading into the velvet
among the other snorts and snickers.

A Collegelands Catechism

Which is known as the 'Orchard County'?
Which as the 'Garden State'?
Which captain of the *Bounty*
was set adrift by his mate?

Who cooked and ate an omelette
midway across Niagara falls?
Where did Setanta get
those magical hurley balls

he ram-stammed down the throat
of the blacksmith's hound?
Why would a Greek philosopher of note
refuse to be bound

by convention but live in a tub
from which he might overhear,
as he went to rub
an apple on his sleeve, the mutineers

plotting to seize the *Maid of the Mist*
while it was still half-able to forge
ahead and make half a fist
of crossing the Niagara gorge,

the tub in which he might light a stove
and fold the beaten
eggs into themselves? Who unearthed the egg-trove?
And who, having eaten

the omelette, would marvel at how the Mounties
had so quickly closed in on him, late
of the 'Orchard County'
by way of the 'Garden State'?

Beagles

That Boxing Day morning, I would hear the familiar, far-
    off gowls and gulders
over Keenaghan and Aughanlig
of a pack of beagles, old dogs disinclined to chase a car
    suddenly quite unlike
themselves, pups coming helter-skelter
across the plowlands with all the chutzpah of veterans
of the trenches, their slate-grays, cinnamons, liver-
    browns, lemons, rusts and violets
turning and twisting, unseen, across the fields,
their gowls and gulders turning and twisting after the
    twists and turns
of the great hare who had just now sauntered into the yard
    where I stood on tiptoe
astride my new Raleigh cycle,
his demeanor somewhat louche, somewhat lackadaisical
under the circumstances, what with him standing on
    tiptoe
as if to mimic me, standing almost as tall as I, looking as
    if he might for a moment put
himself in my place, thinking better of it, sloping off
    behind the lorry-bed.

Tell

He opens the scullery door, and a sudden rush
of wind, as raw as raw,
brushes past him as he himself will brush
past the stacks of straw

that stood in earlier for Crow
or Comanche tepees hung with scalps
but tonight pass muster, row upon row,
for the foothills of the Alps.

He opens the door of the peeling-shed
just as one of the apple-peelers –
one of almost a score
of red-cheeked men who pare

and core
the red-cheeked apples for a few spare
shillings – mutters something about 'bloodshed'
and the 'peelers'.

The red-cheeked men put down their knives
at one and the same
moment. All but his father, who somehow connives
to close one eye as if taking aim

or holding back a tear,
and shoots him a glance
he might take, as it whizzes past his ear,
for another Crow, or Comanche, lance

hurled through the Tilley-lit
gloom of the peeling-shed,
were he not to hear what must be an apple split
above his head.

Guns and Butter

I

It seemed that Bap, who buried two milk-churns
like two zig-zaggy funerary urns
   between the posts of a gate,
would now be most likely to castigate
   me for daring to explode
   the myth of the mother-lode.

II

It seemed that Biscuit, who rigged a tin
of cookies one night in Desertmartin,
   would now hold me in utter
contempt for daring to spread the butter
   meant to save his guns from rust
   on my small bit of a crust.

One Last Draw of the Pipe

Heard a piece of Roscommon folklore the other night. At some
village or other, they lay pipes full of tobacco on the graves of
the new burried in case they may like a draw of the pipe. A wild
American indian kind of buisness it seems.
Letter from W. B. Yeats to Douglas Hyde, October 1889

Even though it happened as long ago as the late fifties, I
    could still draw
you a picture of the place. A little draw

through which we were helping a neighbor draw
green hay when we would suddenly draw

level with a freshly dug hole. He must have been torn
    between one last draw
of the pipe and hurriedly trying to draw

a veil of thatch and pine boughs over the hole before
    having to withdraw,
that ghost who may even now draw

a bead on me. On the day Sitting Bull was shot, his old
    trick pony (once such a draw
in Buffalo Bill's circus because he was given to dance

attendance
when he heard a volley of shots) would automatically
    draw

himself up and raise one hoof.

Even now I hear it coming down. I hear it coming down on my yew-bough roof.

Caedmon's Hymn

Now we must praise to the skies,   the Keeper of the
  heavenly kingdom,
The might of the Measurer,   all he has in mind,
The work of the Father of Glory,   of all manner of marvel,

Our eternal Master,   the main mover.
It was he who first summoned up,   on our behalf,
Heaven as a roof,   the holy Maker.

Then this middle-earth,   the Watcher over humankind,
Our eternal Master,   would later assign
The precinct of men,   the Lord Almighty.

Paul Valéry: *Pomegranates*

Thick-skinned pomegranates, your rinds
forced open by a rashness of seeds, you've led
me to envisage the highest foreheads
bursting with all that comes to mind.

Should all those suns you suffer,
O pomegranates with gaping sides,
leave you so swollen with pride
as to break down your ruby buffers,

should the wizened gold of your skin
give way to pressure from within
and explode in red juice-gems,

that light-shedding fracture
might bring a soul such as I had to dream
of its own hidden architecture.

Pineapples and Pomegranates

In memory of Yehuda Amichai

To think that, as a boy of thirteen, I would grapple
with my first pineapple,
its exposed breast
setting itself as another test
of my will power, knowing in my bones
that it stood for something other than itself alone
while having absolutely no sense
of its being a worldwide symbol of munificence.
Munificence – right? Not munitions, if you understand
where I'm coming from. As if the open hand
might, for once, put paid
to the hand grenade
in one corner of the planet.
I'm talking about pineapples – right? – not pomegranates.

Winter Wheat

I

The plowboy was something his something as I nibbled
 the lobe
of her right ear and something her blouse
for the Empire-blotchy globe
of her left breast on which there something a something
 louse.

II

Those something lice like something seed-pearls
and her collar something with dandruff
as when Queen Elizabeth entertained the Earls
in her something something ruff.

III

I might have something the something groan
of the something plowboy who would with such
 something urge
the something horses, a something and a roan,
had it not been for the something splurge
of something like the hare
which even now managed to something itself from the
 something plowshare.

Herm

In memory of Ted Hughes

He stands in under the hedge, among the sweet-smelling
    flags,
and holds out a white flag
to the distant plow-team
that makes directly for him through the teem

of rain, his head one of those plastered, round stones
atop a heap of pavers and kidney stones.
Or he might be a young holly or ash
what with his brow-beat of ash.

As the team bears down on him through the fertile
meadow, the white on the lead horse's forehead (like the
    white where a tile
once fell off the wall behind the range)
comes into range

and a priest with a handkerchief
reels among those mown down in Derry, whispering to
    him, 'Chief ...'
as he grips his wrist and starts counting,
'We were counting

on you to hold steady, to stay
our consolation and stay.'
'But I've always taken my bearings from *you*,' he'll hear
    himself remark,
'it was you I took for my mark.'

Whitethorns

The paling posts we would tap into the ground with the
    flat of a spade
more than thirty years ago,
hammering them home then with a sledge
and stringing them with wirc to keep our oats from
    Miller's barley,

are maxed-out, multilayered whitethorns, affording us a
    broader, deeper shade
than we ever decently hoped to know,
so far-fetched does it seem, so far-flung from the hedge
under which we now sit down to parley.

Affairs of State

The lock of hair in a green-lined envelope
which was given to me by a woman with whom I planned
  to elope

in the mid-eighties came back, much to my disbelief,
as the single rusty leaf

like a rivet
in a thick hedge of boxwood or privet

along a drive like her front drive, now no more likely to
  disappoint
as it reached its vanishing point

in the hallway's missing tile
like a missing scale on a reptile

than when the previous owner, the diplomat,
had heard a green-lined envelope slither on to the mat

and, picking it up with a little *Oh*,
turned to his wife, the second one, the redhead, shortly to
  be his widow.

The Otter

That was the year S—— told him how on the Queen's
  desk
there lay a great six-by-four-foot blotter
of such a blackness, she would aver,
a blackness so dense
and a grain so close, so compact,
no one could hope to hold
a mirror up to it
and thereby . . . and thereby hit
on any evidence of clandestine contracts or covenants, of
  old
enemies having entered a secret pact
to which she might be a party or affix her hand, any
  evidence
of the treachery he now saw written all over her,
rising as she did to meet him like the otter
that had risen once to meet him from Lough Eske.

John Luke: *The Fox*

Believe you me, when I padded over the plowlands to the
    old Galloway place
I was no less taken aback by the window pane
covered not, as it had first seemed, with Carrickmacross
    lace

but a curtain of frost, than by the painter setting up his
    easel
in a meadow in Clonoe, or Clonmain,
my twitch as his badger and weasel

brushes twitched. Since this was still high summer, since
    the whin
vied with the cylinder of propane
for out-and-out yellowness, I assumed I had no more
    chance of getting in

than had Galloway of getting out, Galloway the
    blacksmith with his crab-claw
of a right arm – as if he'd never had 'but ane' –
Galloway who, in 1912, had stood in line at Balmoral to
    catch a glimpse of Bonar Law.

Anthony Green: *The Second Marriage*

Standing as they do, all primped, primed, pukka, all
    proper, all property-lined, in a room
where every rift's loaded with ore,
they're reminiscent less of a blushing bride and a nervous
    groom
than a pair of con artists summoned before
a magistrate inclined to throw
the book at con artists so that, despite his efforts to
    sustain
the argument that, as distinct from his previous situation
    in Rugby Row,
everything here hinges on his shadow meeting her
    shadow-stain
on the carpet, it looks very much as if, for Mr Stanley
    Joscelyne and his mate,
the case will turn
rather on the provenance of a single inanimate
object – that silver cigarette urn,
it would appear, set on the occasional table
in the center of the room – and the outcome is, as he
    himself would put it, 'inevitable'.

As

As naught gives way to aught
and ox-hide gives way to chain-mail
and byrnie gives way to battle-ax
and Cavalier gives way to Roundhead
and Cromwell Road gives way to the Connaught
and *I Am Curious (Yellow)* gives way to *I Am Curious (Blue)*
and barrelhouse gives way to Frank'n'Stein
and a pint of Shelley plain to a pint of India Pale Ale
I give way to you.

As bass gives way to baritone
and hammock gives way to hummock
and Hoboken gives way to Hackensack
and bread gives way to reed bed
and bald eagle gives way to Theobald Wolfe Tone
and the Undertones give way to Siouxsie Sioux
and DeLorean, John, gives way to Deloria, Vine,
and Pierced Nose to Big Stomach
I give way to you.

As vent gives way to Ventry
and the King of the World gives way to Finn MacCool
and phone gives way to fax
and send gives way to sned
and Dagenham gives way to Coventry
and Covenanter gives way to caribou
and the caribou gives way to the carbine
and Boulud's cackamamie to the cock-a-leekie of Boole
I give way to you.

As transhumance gives way to trance
and shaman gives way to Santa
and butcher's string gives way to vacuum pack
and the ineffable gives way to the unsaid
and pyx gives way to monstrance
and treasure aisle gives way to need-blind pew
and Calvin gives way to Calvin Klein
and Town and Country Mice to Hanta
I give way to you.

As Hopi gives way to Navaho
and rug gives way to rag
and *Pax Vobiscum* gives way to Tampax
and Tampa gives way to the water bed
and *The Water Babies* gives way to *Worstward Ho*
and crapper gives way to loo
and spruce gives way to pine
and the carpet of pine-needles to the carpetbag
I give way to you.

As gombeen-man gives way to not-for-profit
and soft soap gives way to Lynn C. Doyle
and tick gives way to tack
and Balaam's Ass gives way to Mister Ed
and *Songs of Innocence* gives way to *The Prophet*
and single-prop Bar-B-Q gives way to twin-screw
and The Salt Lick gives way to The County Line
and 'Mending Wall' gives way to 'Build Soil'
I give way to you.

As your hummus gives way to your foul madams
and your coy mistress gives way to 'The Flea'
and flax gives way to W. D. Flackes

and the living give way to the dead
and John Hume gives way to Gerry Adams
and Television gives way to U2
and Lake Constance gives way to the Rhine
and the Rhine to the Zuider Zee
I give way to you.

As dutch treat gives way to french leave
and spanish fly gives way to Viagra
and slick gives way to slack
and the local fuzz give way to the Feds
and Machiavelli gives way to make believe
and *Howards End* gives way to *A Room with a View*
and Wordsworth gives way to 'Woodbine
Willie' and stereo Nagra to quad Niagara
I give way to you.

As cathedral gives way to cavern
and cookie cutter gives way to cookie
and the rookies give way to the All Blacks
and the shad give way to the smoke shed
and the rough-shod give way to the Black Horse   avern
that still rings true
despite that 'T' being missing from its sign
where a little nook gives way to a little nookie
when I give way to you.

That *Nanook of the North* should give way to *Man of
    Aran*
as ling gives way to cod
and cod gives way to kayak
and Camp Moosilauke gives way to Club Med
and catamite gives way to catamaran

and catamaran to aluminum canoe
is symptomatic of a more general decline
whereby a cloud succumbs to a clod
and I give way to you.

For as Monet gives way to Juan Gris
and Juan Gris gives way to Joan Miró
and Metro-Goldwyn-Mayer gives way to Miramax
and the Volta gives way to Travolta, swinging the red-hot
   lead,
and *Saturday Night Fever* gives way to *Grease*
and the Greeks give way to you know who
and the Roman IX gives way to the Arabic 9
and nine gives way, as ever, to zero
I give way to you.

The Stoic

This was more like it, looking up to find a burlapped fawn
half-way across the iced-over canal, an Irish navvy who'd
   stood there for an age
with his long-tailed shovel or broad griffawn,
whichever foot he dug with showing the bandage

that saved some wear and tear, though not so much that
   there wasn't a leak
of blood through the linen rag, a red picked up nicely by
   the turban
he sported, those reds lending a little brilliance to the
   bleak
scene of suburban or – let's face it – *urban*

sprawl, a very little brilliance. This was more like the
   afternoon last March
when I got your call in St Louis and, rather than rave
as one might rant and rave at the thought of the yew
from Deirdre's not quite connecting with the yew from
   Naoise's grave,

rather than shudder like a bow of yew or the matchless
   Osage orange
at the thought of our child already lost from view
before it had quite come into range,
I steadied myself under the Gateway Arch

and squinted back, first of all, through an eyelet of bone
to a point where the Souris

had not as yet hooked up with the Assiniboine,
to where the Missouri

had not as yet been swollen by the Osage,
then ahead to where – let's face it – there are now *two*
    fawns
on the iced-over canal, two Irish navvies who've stood
    there for a veritable age
with their long-tailed shovels or broad griffawns.

Famous First Words

Archimedes' first words were 'Stand away from my
diagram.'
Sir Richard Burton's first word was 'Chloroform.'

Chang's first words were 'I don't want to go to bed.'
Alexandre Dumas's first words were 'I shall never know
how it all comes out.'

Thomas Edison's first words were 'It is very beautiful
over there.'
John Ford's first words were 'May I please have a cigar?'

Ulysses S. Grant's first word was 'Water.'
Prince Henry's first words were 'I would say something
but I cannot utter.'

Washington Irving's first words were 'When will this
end?'
James Joyce's first words were 'Does nobody understand?'

Ned Kelly's first words were 'Such is life.'
Saint Lawrence's first words were 'This side is roasted
enough.'

Montezuma's first words were 'I bear you no ill will.'
Scipio Nasica's first words were 'All is well with the
general.'

William Oughtred's first words were 'Are you sure the king is restored?'
Elvis Presley's first words were 'I hope you have not been bored.'

General Alfredo Quijano's first words were 'Still a little closer.'
Maximilien de Robespierre's first words were 'Thank you, sir.'

Gertrude Stein's first words were 'In that case, what's the question?'
Henry David Thoreau's first words were 'Moose ... Indian ...'

Sir Thomas Urquhart's first word was something like 'Habonghadingdonghagong.'
Leonardo da Vinci's first words were 'God and man have I offended.'

William III's first words were 'Can this last long?'
Saint Francis Xavier's first words were 'Let me never be confounded.'

Jack B. Yeats's first words were 'Don't forget your sitting.'
Emile Zola's first words were 'It must be something we've eaten.'

The Grand Conversation

She. My people came from Korelitz
where they grew yellow cucumbers
and studied the Talmud.
He. Mine pored over the mud
of mangold- and potato-pits
or flicked through kale plants from Comber
as bibliomancers of old
went a-flicking through deckle-mold.

She. Mine would lie low in the shtetl
when they heard the distant thunder
stolen by the Cossacks.
He. It was potato-sacks
lumped together on a settle
mine found themselves lying under,
the Peep O'Day Boys from Loughgall
making Defenders of us all.

She. Mine once controlled the sugar trade
from the islets of Langerhans
and were granted the deed
to Charlottesville. *He.* Indeed?
My people called a spade a spade
and were admitted to the hanse
of pike- and pickax-men, shovels
leaning to their lean-to hovels.

She. Mine were trained to make a suture
after the bomb and the bombast

have done their very worst.
He. Between *fearsad* and *verst*
we may yet construct our future
as we've reconstructed our past
and cry out, my love, each to each
from his or her own quicken-queach.

She. Each from his stand of mountain ash
will cry out over valley farms
spot-lit with pear blossom.
He. There some young Absalom
picks his way through cache after cache
of ammunition and small arms
hidden in grain-wells, while his nag
tugs at a rein caught on a snag.

On

Absalom was riding his mule and the mule passed under the
thick branches of a great oak. Absalom's head got caught in the
oak and he was left hanging between heaven and earth, while
the mule he was riding went on.

II Samuel 18:9

I make my way alone through the hand-to-hand fighting
to A3 and A5. Red velvet. Brass and oak.
The special effects will include strobe lighting
and artificial smoke.

A glance to A5. Patrons are reminded, *mar bheadh*,
that the management accepts no responsibility in the
    case of theft.
Even as the twenty-five-piece orchestra
that's masked offstage left

strikes up, there's still a chance, I suppose, that the
    gainsayers
might themselves be gainsaid
as you rush, breathless, into my field of vision.

Understudies and standbys never substitute for listed
    players,
however, unless a specific announcement is made.
There will be no intermission.

An Old Pit Pony

An old pit pony walks
its chalks
across a blasted heath.

Its coat is a cloud hung on a line.

It sighs
for the pit-propped skies
of that world beneath.

Its coat is a cloud hung on a line.

Summer Coal

I   *Griggstown, June 1889*

Always the fence, always the row of bottles
lining the fence at the end of a garden
that runs down to the canal. From where we stand, on the
  barge,
it's like looking through a curtain

of magenta glass, or saffron with snuff-mottles,
or cobalt, or viridian,
in which a cottage now puckers, now is large
as life. We close one eye and think of our good fortune

compared to theirs, glad to know
we might as easily get the measure
of them as we do their bottles left for show

on a silver-gray cedar pole,
steadying ourselves and picking them off at our leisure
with lumps of coal.

II   *Griggstown, June 1889*

It's like looking through a chink in wattle
and daub that has yet to harden,
through a scrim of feldspar-loaded sparge,
as two mule tenders come along the Delaware and
  Raritan

at something approaching full throttle.
These are mule tenders of my own age, thirteen or
    fourteen,
who may yet be conscripted to lead a charge
against Villa, to fall at Vimy or Verdun,

so eagerly they throw
themselves into their work. Little do they suspect that
    the pleasure
they take in their slow

bombardment might be surpassed by our own, as we fill
    the cellar hole
in which we store such treasure
with lumps of coal.

The Loaf

When I put my finger to the hole they've cut for a dimmer
    switch
in a wall of plaster stiffened with horsehair
it seems I've scratched a two-hundred-year-old itch

with a pink and a pink and a pinkie-pick.

When I put my ear to the hole I'm suddenly aware
of spades and shovels turning up the gain
all the way from Raritan to the Delaware

with a clink and a clink and a clinky-click.

When I put my nose to the hole I smell the flood-plain
of the canal after a hurricane
and the spots of green grass where thousands of Irish have
    lain

with a stink and a stink and a stinky-stick.

When I put my eye to the hole I see one holding horse
    dung to the rain
in the hope, indeed, indeed,
of washing out a few whole ears of grain

with a wink and a wink and a winkie-wick.

And when I do at last succeed
in putting my mouth to the horsehair-fringed niche
I can taste the small loaf of bread he baked from that
  whole seed

with a link and a link and a linky-lick.

The Outhouse

This would have been a night in late August,
somewhere in or around the turn of the century, when a
    little gust
bestirred itself from Lake Champlain
and he himself got up, as a dead man might get up, from
    where he'd lain

to find his way over that ever-treacherous rise
in the yard. Some version of the outhouse still stood and –
    surprise, surprise –
as he unbuttoned himself to answer this 'call of nature'
he found himself staring straight at his own majuscule
    signature.

What with the slightly unhinged seat, the spiked news
    stories, the dead-dog scent
of lilac, the lemon-lye, what with the acidic and the
    alkaline
muddling on into one odor,

he knew in his bones that the crescent
moon would, for once, align
itself with the crescent moon cut high in the long-gone
    outhouse door.

News Headlines from the Homer Noble Farm

I

That case-hardened cop.
A bull moose in a bog-hole
brought him to a stop.

II

From his grassy knoll
he has you in his cross-hairs,
the accomplice mole.

III

This sword once a share.
This forest a fresh-faced farm.
This stone once a stair.

IV

The birch crooks her arm,
as if somewhat more inclined
to welcome the swarm.

V

He has, you will find,
two modes only, the chipmunk:
fast forward; rewind.

VI

The smell, like a skunk,
of coffee about to perk.
Thelonious Monk.

VII

They're the poker work
of some sort of woodpecker,
these holes in the bark.

VIII

My new fact-checker
claims that *pilus* means 'pestle'.
My old fact-checker.

IX

The Rose and Thistle.
Where the hummingbird drops in
to wet his whistle.

X

Behind the wood bin
a garter snake snaps itself,
showing us some skin.

XI

Like most bits of delf,
the turtle's seen at its best
on one's neighbor's shelf.

XII

Riding two abreast
on their stripped-down, souped-up bikes,
bears in leather vests.

XIII

The eye-shaded shrike.
BIRD BODIES BURIED IN BOG'S
a headline he'll spike.

XIV

Steady, like a log
riding a sawmill's spill-way,
the steady coydog.

XV

The cornet he plays
was Bolden's then Beiderbecke's,
this lonesome blue jay.

XVI

Some fresh auto wreck.
Slumped over a horn. Sump pool.
The frog's neck-braced neck.

XVII

Brillo pads? Steel wool?
The regurrrrrrrrrrrrrrrrrrrrrgitations, what,
of a long-eared owl?

XVIII

The jet with the jot.
The drive-in screen with the sky.
The blood with the blot.

XIX

How all seems to vie,
not just my sleeping laptop
with the first firefly.

The Killdeer

Why was he trying to clear
a space in the forest of beech
by turning beech posts and, by beech pegs,
fitting each to each?

For the reason at which the killdeer
seems to be clutching
when she lays her four pear-shaped eggs
with the pointed ends touching.

Horace: *Two Odes*

While the young herdsman, Paris, a herdsman as faithless
    as he was fair,
was hauling Helen back on his boat
of Trojan pine, the sea-god Nereus would stop the sea-airs
that can't abide being stopped and float

this vision of the future: 'It doesn't bode well that you've
    taken on deck
a woman whom the Greeks will band together and swear
    an oath
to recover by force, determined as they'll be to wreck
your marriage and old Priam's kingdom both,

and I dread to think of the sweat-drenched horses, the
    men drenched with sweat,
dread to think of the carnage
you're visiting on Troy. Even now Athena is laying out
    her breastplate and helmet,
limbering up her battle carriage and battle rage.

However confident you may be about coming under
    Venus's special care,
there'll be no point in pretending to groom
your long hair while from your measured lyre you pluck
    the measured airs
the ladies seem to go for. There'll be no point in hiding
    out in the bedroom

to avoid the heavy throwing-spears and Cretan arrowheads,
what with Ajax hard on your heels, what with the
   rumpus and ruck
of battle. Then you may dread
to think, after all, of your long hair dragged through the
   muck.

Can't you make out Ulysses, sworn enemy of your
   people, at your back?
Nestor of Pylos coming after you?
Teucer of Salamis hot on your tracks?
Not to speak of Sthenelus, who knows a thing or two

about handling himself in a fight, not to speak
of handling a chariot team.
Meriones is yet another Greek
with whom you'll be all too familiar. Diomedes also,
   whom some deem

deadlier than his father, Tydeus, is following in your wake,
and when you sight him, like a stag sighting a wolf on the
   opposite hillside,
you'll soon forget grass nibbling and take off, head thrown
   back, breathless, all aquake –
hardly what she thought was coming to her, your bride.

For though Achilles and his fleet, consumed as they are
   with ire,
may delay the course of events, by the time ten years have
   rolled round
the Greeks will have set the fire
that will burn Troy to the ground.'

Faunus, you who love the nymphs, from whom the
    nymphs love to run,
may you look kindly, as you cross in and out of my farm,
on its boundary posts and pastures already blessed by the
    sun,
and deliver the littlest of my flock from harm

if it please you that, at the high point of the year,
a little kid might indeed be offered to you, the wine
which Venus holds so dear
indeed fill the mixing bowl, smoke rise from the ancient
    shrine,

one and all besporting themselves on the still-green
    grazing
as early December rolls round, be it the flocks
of sheep or the country folk lazing
with the lazing ox,

the wolf moving among lambs remarkable for their
    nonchalance,
the trees putting out their red
carpet for you, or the ditch-digger dancing a three-step
    victory dance
on the earth with which he's gone head-to-head.

Eugenio Montale: *The Eel*

The self-same, the siren
of icy waters, shrugging off as she does the Baltic
to hang out in our seas,
our inlets, the rivers
through which she climbs, bed-hugger, who keeps going
    against
the flow, from branch to branch, then
from capillary to snagged capillary,
farther and farther in, deeper and deeper into the heart
of the rock, straining
through mud runnels, till one day
a flash of light from the chestnut trees
sends a fizzle through a standing well,
through a drain that goes
by dips and darts from the Apennines to the Romagna –
that self-same eel, a firebrand now, a scourge,
the arrow-shaft of Love on earth
which only the gulches or dried-out
gullies of the Pyrenees might fetch and ferry back
to some green and pleasant spawning ground,
a green soul scouting and scanning
for life where only
drought and desolation have hitherto clamped down,
the spark announcing
that all sets forth when all that's set forth
is a charred thing, a buried stump,
this short-lived rainbow, its twin met
in what's set there between your eyelashes,

you who keep glowing as you do, undiminished, among
   the sons
of man, faces glistening with your slime, can't you take in
her being your next-of-kin?

When Aifric and I Put In at that Little Creek

When Aifric and I put in at that little creek
in the shadow of Masatiompan
what struck me most was not the view. What struck me
    most
was the reek
as from the copper pan

her father would pore over each and every morning, the
    ravel
of straw-strain and honey-strand
as he leaned against the tiller post
and winced at his own kidney gravel.
When our little boat lurched toward the strand

Aifric herself lurched, and I was fortunate in being able,
on account of the riding up of her Aran
sweater that seemed to boast
not only 'diamond' and 'cable'
but 'basket' stitches, to glimpse the spot where the colors
    ran

red and black. For though our sonar was pretty much state
    of the art,
the truth is that we had found our way back
along this coast
largely by means of the chart
her father had drawn and redrawn on Aifric's back

with nothing more than a bronze pin
and lamp-soot and red ochre, the constant twinge and
  tweak
of detail with which he had been so engrossed
when he suddenly caught the swing of the boom and took
  that fatal spin
only the previous week.

The Ancestor

The great-grandmother who bears down on us, as if
    beholding the mote
in our eye, from a nineteenth-century Hungarian portrait
on our library wall is no relation. Not even remote.
The straw-hatted man in a daguerreotype, though he and I
    may share the trait

of putting two fingers to the little carbuncle
on our right chin, is no more of my blood than I am
consanguineous with Cromwell. Our *Webster's* is
    inscribed 'Philip. Best uncle.'
Our napkins bear an unfamiliar monogram.

Yet how familiar all become. Shaving mug, gymkhana
    rosette, five charms
from a charm bracelet – all those heirlooms
to which we're now the heirs are at once more
    presentable and

more present than our own. This great-grandmother with
    folded arms
who lurches and looms
across the library may not be so unreasoning in her
    reprimand.

Homesickness

The lion stretched like a sandstone lion on the sandstone
  slab
of a bridge with one fixture, a gaslight,
looks up from his nicotine-worried forepaw
with the very same air my father, Patrick,
had when the results came back from the lab,
that air of anguish-awe
that comes with the realization of just how slight
the chances are of anything doing the trick

as the sun goes down over Ballyknick and Ballymacnab
and a black-winged angel takes flight.

The black-winged angel leaning over the sandstone
  parapet
of the bridge wears a business suit, dark gray.
His hair is slick with pomade.
He turns away as my mother, Brigid,
turned away not only from her sandstone pet
but any concession being made.
The black-winged angel sets her face to the unbending
  last ray
of evening and meets rigid with rigid

as the sun goes down over Lisnagat and Listamlet
and Clonmore and Clintyclay.

Feckless as he was feckless, as likely as her to be in a
    foofaraw,
I have it in me to absolutely rant and rail while, for fear of
    the backlash,
absolutely renounce
the idea of holding anything that might be construed as
    an opinion.
The lion still looks back to his raw
knuckle and sighs for the possibility that an ounce
of Walnut plug might shape up from the ash.
The angel still threatens to abandon us with a single flick
    of her pinion

as the sun goes down over Lislasly and Lissaraw
and Derrytrasna and Derrymacash.

Two Stabs at Oscar

I

As I roved out between a gaol
and a river in spate
in June as like as January
I happened on a gate
which, though it lay wide open,
would make me hesitate.

I was so long a prisoner
that, though I now am free,
the thought that I serve some sentence
is so ingrained in me
that I still wait for a warder
to come and turn the key.

II

A stone breaker on his stone bed
lay no less tightly curled
than opposite-leaved saxifrage
that even now, unfurled,
has broken through its wall of walls
into this other world.

The Breather

Think of this gravestone
as a long, low chair
strategically placed
at a turn in the stair.

The Goose

When Hermes gave that bit of a goose to the goose farmer
it not only laid an egg
packed with gold but its leg
was a scaled-down version of a knight's in armor,

its beak done in a pinch
of gold so fine it might have been beaten by some master
    gilder
described by Pliny the Elder,
give or take a thousandth of an inch.

II

About as deep, then, as the melanoma
they diagnosed in one old friend, so taking it upon
    themselves to dig
a hole in her as long as the main street in Omagh.

III

As if they hadn't already made enough room –
for *whatever* it is – when they went after another's
    ovaries and womb.
Yesterday she drove down to Newry to buy a bit of a wig.

A Brief Discourse on Decommissioning

I stood between Biscuit and Bap
  in the mortar-mixed gap
to the field where they put the lid
  on that great pyramid
we'd built about a musket-stack
  as Bap laid down the law:
you can't make bricks without the straw
  that breaks the camel's back.

The Turn

In those days when the sands
might shift at any moment, when his mother might at
   any moment lay
into him, he thought nothing of getting up half-way
   through a story about the Sahara,
the one about the tribesman following the scent
of water to a water hole, thought nothing of getting up
   and going out
while he was still half-way through a sentence, going out
   and taking a turn

about the house, sometimes not bothering to return
for an hour, two hours, a week, a year perhaps, perhaps
   not until the sands
of time had run out,
not until his favorite guinea hen had brought herself to
   lay
a double-yolked egg, or the double scent
of the sand-pile and the dunghill made a Sahara

of the yard through which Ned Skinner had moaned
   'Saahaara, Saahaara',
the yard in which, after seeing *The Four Feathers*, he'd
   taken it upon himself to turn
a stack of pear boxes still redolent of the scent
of pears into a bolster-humped camel that carried him
   across the endless sands
to where Harry Feversham and himself lay
in wait in a gully for the last of those out-and-out

cowards and scoundrels, the yard in which he'd not only
    learned to spout
most, if not all, of the main languages of the Sahara
but had such a grasp of the lay
of the land, every twist and turn
of the ergs and regs which looked for all the world like
    featureless sands,
had so mastered following the scent

of water to a water hole, shielding his eyes from the hen
    house's fluorescent
strip of light, under which he could make out a couple
    making out
in a featureless room in the old Sands,
or a featureless room in the Sahara,
a light by which he could make out every twist and turn
in what would have seemed to a lay

person a featureless hotel room, a room which offered
    him an instant replay
of the old bolster and pear-box scent
rising from the camel under him, a scent powerful
    enough to turn
him around, reminding him that he'd already been out
for an hour, two hours, a week, a year perhaps, having
    him turn back through the Sahara
in which so many had perished, back through the sands

on which lay the bones of thousands
of his countrymen, through the sand-pile that was not at
    all reminiscent of the Sahara,
having him turn back inside to pick up his own sentence,
    to hear himself out.

Redknots

The day our son is due is the very day
the redknots are meant to touch down
on their long haul
from Chile to the Arctic Circle,
where they'll nest on the tundra
within a few feet
of where they were hatched.
Forty or fifty thousand of them
are meant to drop in along Delaware Bay.

They time their arrival on these shores
to coincide with the horseshoe crabs
laying their eggs in the sand.
Smallish birds to begin with,
the redknots have now lost half their weight.
Eating the eggs of the horseshoe crabs
is what gives them the strength to go on,
forty or fifty thousand of them getting up all at once
as if for a rock concert encore.

Cradle Song for Asher

When they cut your birth cord yesterday
it was I who drifted away.

Now I hear your name (in Hebrew, 'blest')
as yet another release of ballast

and see, beyond your wicker
gondola, camp-fires, cities, whole continents flicker.

At the Sign of the Black Horse, September 1999

Awesome, the morning after Hurricane Floyd, to sit out
  in our driveway and gawk
at yet another canoe or kayak
coming down Canal Road, now under ten feet of water.
  We've wheeled to the brim
the old Biltrite pram
in which, wrapped in a shawl of Carrickmacross
lace and a bonnet
of his great-grandmother Sophie's finest needlepoint,
Asher sleeps on, as likely as any of us to find a way across

the millrace on which logs (trees more than logs)
are borne along, to which the houses down by the old
  Griggstown Locks
have given up their inventory.
I'm happy for once to be left high and dry,
happy that the house I may yet bring myself to call mine
is set on a two-hundred-and-fifty-year-old slab,
happy that, if need be, we might bundle a few belongings
  into a pillow slip
and climb the hill and escape, Please Examine

Your Change, to a place where the soul might indeed
  recover
radical innocence. A police launch maneuvering by
  brought back troops on maneuver,
some child-kin of my children dipping a stale
crust in his bowl of kale
while listening to his parents complain about the cost

of running a household
in the Poland of the 1930s, the child who, Please Hold,
a peaked cap would shortly accost

for the whereabouts of his uncle, the sofer.
Awesome, however stormy yesterday's weather, to
   calmly don a safari
hat that somewhat matches my safari coat
and, determined as I am to make the most of the power
   cut
here on Ararat,
tear another leaf from Edward Bulwer-Lytton's
King Poppy to light the barbecue, the barbecue shortly to
   be laden
with Dorothy's favorite medallions of young rat

and white-lipped peccary taken this morning not with
   old-fashioned piano wire
but the latest in traps. I'll rake the ashes of the fire
on which they'll cook, No Turn
On Red, and watch the Mediterranean
do its level best to meet the 'Caribbon',
as Dorothy pronounced it once, on Canal Road, No Way
   Out,
having taken down from the attic the ancient Underwood
with the one remaining black ribbon

and set up shop in a corner of the garage.
When we wheeled the old Biltrite baby carriage
to the brink this morning, I was awestruck to see in
   Asher's glabrous
face a slew of interlopers

not from Maghery, as I might have expected, or Maghera,
　　or Magherafelt
(though my connections there are now few and far
　　between),
but the likes of that kale-eating child on whom the
　　peaked cap, *Verboten*,
would shortly pin a star of yellow felt,

having accosted him on the Mosaic
proscription, Please Secure Your Own Oxygen Mask
Before Attending To Children, on the eating of white-
　　lipped peccary.
Just one step ahead of the police launch, meanwhile, a
　　1920 Studebaker
had come down Canal Road, Do Not Fill
Above This Line, carrying another relative, Arnold
　　Rothstein, the brain
behind the running, during Prohibition, of grain
alcohol into the States, his shirt the very same Day-Glo
　　green of chlorophyll

on the surface of a cattle bath
or the canal itself, the canal that ordinarily reflects berm
　　bank and tow-path
as calm as calm. Jean had been fixing Asher a little gruel
from leftover cereal
and crumbled Zwieback
when Uncle Arnie came floating by the 'nursery'.
This was the Arnold Rothstein who had himself fixed the
　　1919 World Series
by bribing eight Chicago White Sox players, Keep Back

Fifty Feet, to throw the game. So awestruck were we by
   his Day-Glo
shirt we barely noticed how low
in the water his Studebaker lay, the distribution of its
   cargo of grain alcohol
(filtered through a makeshift charcoal-
packed, double downspout
by an accomplice, Waxey Gordon) somewhat less than
   even.
'The peccary's hind foot,' the peaked cap would enquire,
   'you call that *cloven*?'
Asher slept on, his little pout

set off beautifully by the pillow case
into which we might yet bundle the foul madams, the
   couscous,
the tabouleh carry-out
full of grit
from the Sahara, while Uncle Arnie had taken his
   lawyer's advice,
maintaining that he paid none of the eight White Sox
who stood in the witness box
as much as a nickel. Racketeering, maybe. Extortion,
   maybe. Maybe vice.

But not throwing games. It wasn't an area in which he
   had expertise. Not an expert.
Isaac Wolf of New Haven, meanwhile, had unzipped
a freezer bag and made a dent
in the defrosted dough in which we'd meant
to wrap the loin of peccary, Please Use Tongs,
in an Aussie version of the secret

recipe the Duke of Wellington had secured
from the Killadar of Perinda, one which substituted
   quantongs

for apricots. While Asher slept on, half hid
under the cradle hood,
his great-grandfather Jim Zabin, an ad-man who held, of
   all things, the Biltrite account,
Please Examine Your Change As Mistakes Cannot,
nodded from his death-bed to the red
stain on the muslin cloth
that covered the peccary in its autoclave
as if that cloth were an obstacle whereby the haystack-
   and roof-leveling wind, bred

on the Atlantic, might at last
be stayed. 'By which authority,' another great-
   grandfather, Sam Korelitz, would blast
from his hardware store in Lawrence, Mass., 'did you
   deny Asher a bris?'
A chainsaw had let rip. Our next-door neighbor, Bruce,
was making quite a hand
of amputating a sycamore limb that had given its all
to the wind and rain. Asher slept on, his shawl
of Carrickmacross lace, his bonnet tied with silk reputed
   to come from Samarkhand,

while Dorothy stood where the Delaware and Raritan
   Canal and the Millstone
River combined to carry ton upon ton
of clay, hay, hair, shoes, spectacles, Please Use The
   Hammer To Break
The Glass, playing ducks and drakes

with the child-kin shortly to be riven
from her family and I, the so-called Goy from the Moy,
scrubbed the trap made in Marengo, Illinois,
by which we took that white-lipped peccary, as if
    scrubbing might leave me shriven.

A flicker from behind Asher's sleeping lids, all covered
    with little wheals and whelks,
as Jean's distant cousin, Helene Hanff, began to rub a mix
    of cumin and baby talc
(cornstarch more than talc) into another loin
of peccary, this being a trick Helene
had picked up from the individual who started a trend
by keeping a rabbit warren-
cum-dovecote in a mews off Charing Cross Road, Hard
    Hats Must Be Worn,
an individual who picked it up from whichever Waugh
    deemed a pram in the hallway the end

of art, a Waugh who could no doubt trace it back to
    Wellington and the Killadar
of Perinda. I looked up in dismay as the helter-skelter
I'd raised in lieu of a lonely tower (part float, part floating
    derrick)
was nudged by the millrace. The increasingly eccentric
Helene, meanwhile, continued to rub
cornstarch into the remains
of whatever curled in the autoclave. Almost inaudible
    now, the sycamore moans
as, almost inaudibly, I myself continued to scrub

the latest in traps with a wire brush
from Sam's hardware store in Lawrence, Mass. 'You
    ignore the Midrash
by which authority?' I could hear small incendiary
devices going off in the midst of the pleasantries
exchanged at this, as every, family gathering, Please Do
    Not Leave Window Ajar,
where the stricken
face of Uncle Arnie's friend Fanny Brice peeked from her
    astrakhan.
'According to Horace,' Arnie maintained, 'every water
    pitcher started out as a wine jar.

You may take Fanny for a nincompoop,
but I fear she may well be the only one here who's
    actually read *King Poppy*.
I fear, moreover, the way the smoke flings
and flails itself from your barbecue brings back that
    terrible morning, in Sing Sing,
they fried Charlie Becker.' Helene looked up from her
    cumin
splitting while Bruce began to pulverize
a stand of young sassafras
with all the zeal of a chainsaw catechumen

and the groundbreaking Irish navvies continued to keen
    and kvetch
through the hole cut for a dimmer switch
in a wall of deh-dah stiffened with deh-dah. Next to moor
his little punt at our dock was Joe Hanff, the banker who
    helped Louis B. Mayer
and Thomas Edison develop a 'cool' projection lamp.
    Where he'd come by the Coke and bucket

of popcorn God only knows.
He handed them to Dorothy for safekeeping while he
    concentrated on the minutiae
of the peccary trap and the great trebucket

with which we've been known to take even larger critters,
setting and upsetting the trebucket as would an obsessive
    compulsive, Out Of Order,
until he was himself ousted by Sam,
Sam who repeated the opening phrase (' 'asherey ha'ish
    'asher') of the Book of Psalms
as he handed Asher a Berbecker and Rowland
upholstery nail which Asher held as grim as grim
while sleeping on. Ton upon ton of clay, hay, hair, shoes
    and spectacle frames
made it less and less likely that we would land

on our feet on the Griggstown Causeway any time soon,
    Ramp Divides,
Please Examine Your Change As Mistakes Cannot Be
    Rectified,
the almost inaudible roar
of the millrace drowning out a great-grandfather's prayer.
By which authority did we deny Asher a mohel?
By which authority did we deny Asher a rebe?
Asher, meanwhile, slept on, his most crape-creepered of
    cribs
riding out the torrent, riding out the turmoil

of those thousands of Irish navvies piling clay, hay, hair
    into their creels
and bearing them at shoulder height, or above, with all
    the zeal

of creel catechumens. A tattoo on the left forearm
of some child-kin of my children, a very faint tattoo.
    Once more the storm
was howling and something, deh-dah, deh-dah,
something about that clay and hair going down the sluice
brought back an afternoon in St Louis.
Something about raking the ashes of the barbecue at the
    end of the verandah

and turning over the loin and flank
of a young peccary, its loin so lean and lank,
its little rib-cage, Road Narrows.
Something about turning over that runt of the peccary
    farrow,
with a dink and a dink
and a dinky-dick, brought back that afternoon.
    Something about Sam lighting a menorah
and reading a commentary on the Torah,
something about Arnie distancing himself from the
    'night-and-fog' of Murder Inc.

to a disbelieving Duke of Wellington and Killadar of
    Perinda,
brought back the day
of our own *Nacht-und-Nebel Erlass*
on which I'd steadied myself under the Gateway Arch and
    pondered the loss
of our child. It was Arnie who'd been the brain behind
    running rum
to those thousands of Irish schlemiels
who dug the canal. A flicker from Asher's lids. The little
    whelks and wheals.
As if he might be dreaming of a Pina Colostrum

on Boscobel Beach, some young beauty dipping his foot in
    Johnson's baby oil.
Fanny peeked from her astrakhan, its poile
the poile of a stillborn lamb. Again a chainsaw letting rip.
Again I scrubbed the very latest in traps
while Helene rubbed cornstarch into whatever was
    curled, rawer and rawer,
in the autoclave. 'That peccary with the hind foot,'
the peaked cap would enquire, 'it's a bad case of *spina
    bifida*?'
I heard a bottom drawer

open somewhere. The red stain on the lint
that covered whatever it was in the autoclave brought
    back an afternoon in Poland
when the smoke would flail and fling itself, Maximum
    Headroom,
from a crematorium
at Auschwitz. It was not without some
trepidation, so, that I trained my camcorder
on this group of creel carters
bearing clay, hay, hair (at shoulder height, or above)
    through the awesome

morning after Hurricane Floyd as yet another 1921 Benz
    or 1924 Bugatti
came down Canal Road and yet another peaked
cap was enquiring of my child-kin the meaning of
    '*Ashkenaz*',
Place Mask Over Mouth and Nose,
my trepidation becoming more and more
pronounced as that smoke would flail and fling itself over
    Auschwitz.

I looked up from our make-believe version of Boscobel
    Beach
to a cauterized stump of sassafras or sycamore

as the creel carters piled more and more clay, hay, hair,
    spectacle frames, *Willkommen*,
on to the line of carrioles and camions
by the edge of the flooded stream, those creel carters
    imagining in excited reverie
the arches of the bridge wrought with the motto *Arbeit
    Macht Frei*,
while I looked up through the swing
and swale of smoke, Please Leave A Message After The
    Beep,
and watched the kebab-babby we had lost a year or two
    back put on its best bib
and tucker, watched it put out its little bit of a wing

all tinged with char
as if to set off for the real Boscobel Beach (on which we
    had met Sandra Hughes and Anton Hajjar),
oblivious to the piles of hair, spectacle frames, bootees
    and brogans
borne along from wherever. 'The full name is Auschwitz-
    Birkenau,'
Sam was explaining to Anton and Sandra,
who had somehow summoned themselves. Asher slept
    on, of course, despite his thrush,
despite his diaper rash,
the flood water having receded from the point on the
    driveway at which the pachysandra

had earlier been swamped, the point at which Arnie had
    fixed some class of a tow rope
to the chassis of the Studebaker. 'I simply don't have it in
    me to bribe
a ballplayer,' he would main-
tain, steadying himself with a handful of mane
as he hooked the rope to the hames of a draft mule, This
    Truck
Makes Wide Right Turns. The fact that the slew of
    interlocutors
in Asher's glabrous face now included, of all things, the
    peccary runt, Do Not Litter,
left me no less awestruck

than if the Studebaker were to be suddenly yanked back
    to the factory in South Bend
from which it had been packed off, Open This End,
than if the soul of one of the dozen stillborn
lambs sewn into Fanny's astrakhan were to recover
    radical innocence and learn,
than if scouring the trap by which I had taken that
    peccary, so lank and lean,
by its dinky hind leg,
Don't Walk, than if, Don't Walk, than if, Don't Walk,
than if scouring might make it clean.

An overwhelming sense of déjà vu. The creel caravan
swaying along the salt route into Timbuktu. Fanny
    taking up a hand-held microphone
and embarking on 'Secondhand Rose'. The convoy
of salt merchants setting down their loys
at one and the same moment. Our piliated woodpecker
    tapping at the bark

of three successive sycamores in the hope of finding one
   in tune.
The piles of clay, hay, hair, spectacle frames, hand-me-
   down
bootees and brogans now loaded on to the ark

causing it to lie so much lower in the water that Uncle
   Arnie gives a heavy hint
to Fanny that she should cut the chorus of 'Secondhand
Rose' and jump ship. 'The whitewall
tire,' Helene concurs, 'is the beginning of the pram in the
   hall.'
Asher sleeps on, attended by two Teddy bears,
his soul less likely than ever to recover radical innocence
   and learn at last
that it is self-delighting. Ada Korelitz, Sam's widow, is
   drawing up A-, B-, and C-lists
of the Korelitz forebears

whom she'll invite to a reception thrown by herself and
   Arnie, Unapproved Road,
for the 1919 World Series-winning Cincinnati Reds.
'If there's no hatred in a mind,' Isaac Wolf
pounds and expounds, 'assault and battery of the wind
   can never tear the deh-dah from the leaf.'
'As for the killdeer,' Helene peeks from an astrakhan
   almost as natty
as Fanny's, 'you're thinking, in all likelihood,
of the killdeer of Perinda.' The ark now lies so much
   lower in the water, Stop Ahead,
that Uncle Arnie gives another heavy hint to the
   Cincinnati

Reds that they should also jump ship, *Achtung*.
The 1920 Studebaker's just one step ahead of a Panther
    tank
nodding approvingly through the ghetto after the
    Germans have massacred
the Jews of Bialystok. The wind bred on the Atlantic has
    broken Belmar and Seagirt.
Boundbrook is broken. The roof-leveling wind, profane
    and irreverent,
the wind which was at the spearhead
of the attack on the ark, almost inaudible. The memory of
    a three-month growth spurt
no more than a flicker, For Rent,

behind Asher's sleeping lids. The A-, B-, and C-lists of
    forebears in his glabrous face.
Hanff. Wolf. Reinhart. Abrams. A Reinhart beginning to
    fuss
as a peaked cap enquires about the Orthodox
position on the eating of white-lipped peccary. The train
    stopped in Bialystok's
running neither to Warsaw nor Leningrad.
Helene uttering a little cuss
as the yellow of that star brings back the out-and-out
    yellowness of a cylinder of gas
she once saw on Charing Cross Road. Now Isaac Wolf, a
    Yale grad,

looks on helplessly at the millrace on which sign-post,
    sign-board, Birdseed, Keep Out,
Bridge Freezes Before Road, Do Not Drive In Breakdown
    Lane, Live Bait,
my lonely helter-skelter, $500 Fine,

the makeshift oven
in which we meant, Keep Clear, All Directions, the
    Vermont decal
on that Bugatti-load of grain alcohol, Slow,
the out-and-out yellow
of the sign-post that points toward the place where the
    soul might recover radical

innocence, No Stopping Except For Repairs, the
    makeshift oven in which we meant to bake
the peccary *en croute*, Contents Under Pressure, the
    freezer bag
into which we've bundled the carry-out from the Sahara,
the sign-post that points to where the Missouri
had not as yet been swollen, Hump, No Shoulder, No Rail,
are all borne along, Toll Booth,
to where Uncle Arnie's father, Abraham Rothstein, one of
    the founders of Beth
Israel (ycs, *Beth Israel*),

joins Fanny Brice in the version of 'My Man' she first sang
    in the Ziegfeld Follies.
A flicker from behind the lids. As if those children-kin
    might flee
as they fled the Cossacks in the Ukraine,
Please Remember To Take Your Belongings When You
    Leave The Train,
woken as they now are by a piliated Rowland and Berbecker
tapping into a sycamore. Asher's face a fox's mask
nailed to a long-gone door-post by an Irish schlemiel as
    likely as not to mosk
his brogans for a ladle of rum. 'What's with these police
    captains, like Charlie Becker,'

Arnie puts his arm around Helene, who, being chosen,
    finds life flat,
Contents May Have Shifted During Flight,
'who think they're above the law, who think they're born
    without belly buttons?'
The police launch maneuvering by brings back riot
    shields and batons,
some child-kin of my children picking at his kohlrabi.
Now Helene leaves off rubbing cornstarch
into the arch
of whatever lies in the autoclave, sets the little beak of
    her Colibri

wobblingly to a cigarette, Pull To Open,
and reaches into a drawer for the poultry shears. The
    hacking through a babby bone.
No obstacle but Gregory's wood
and one bare hill, Slippery When Wet,
bringing back the morning Dr Patel had systematically
    drawn
the child from Jean's womb, For Hire,
Uncle Arnie all the while hanging a whitewall tire
about the draft mule's neck, the draft mule no less
    thraward-thrawn

than whichever Waugh deemed the pram in the hallway
    the end of art.
The peaked cap sweet-talking that young Abrams or
    Reinhart
with the offer of a tin of waffeletten
should he feel able to enlighten
him on the particular house in the Bialystok ghetto

in which his uncle is hunkering down. Asher puts his lips
   to the shofar
of a long-gone pacifier
as Isaac Wolf expounds to Fanny Brice ('it's from *getto*, "a
   foundry", not *borghetto*,

a "borough" '), on that little gore, that little gusset
of ground into which my cast
of thousands of Irish schmucks have been herded, *Halt*.
Asher opens his eyes. Once more the storm is howling as
   it howled
when Isaac shouted down the board of Yale, the Black
   Horse Tavern still served ale,
when Sophie was found dead in the bath, a ringed plover
with all her rings stolen, Please Cover,
when Sam discontinued his line of Berbecker and
   Rowland upholstery nails, For Sale,

when we might yet have climbed the hill and escaped by
   Coppermine,
when Uncle Arnie was gut-shot (by George McManus?)
for non-payment of tight-lipped, poker-faced debts, when
   Helene Hanff, the celeb,
was found asleep
in the De Witt nursing home in the arms of Bulwer-
   Lytton, Follow Detour,
when Fanny tried to stop the leak
of a so-called confession by one Joseph Gluck
which fingered her ex-husband, Nicky Arnstein, when
   the trebucket of my lonely *túr*

was tripped for the very last time by Joe Hanff, No Egress,
when a cantankerous

young Reinhart or Abrams, No Children Beyond This
Point,
was borne along at shoulder height by the peaked cap,
Out Of Bounds,
when the cry went up from a starving Irish schlemiel who
washed an endosperm
of wheat, deh-dah, from a pile of horse-keek
held to the rain, one of those thousands of Irish schmucks
who still loll, still loll and lollygag,
between the preposterous tow-path and the preposterous
berm.